BIRTH OF A POET:

The Prison Letters of Justin Booth

Edited by Marcia Camp

Cowboy Buddha Publishing, LLC

Birth of A Poet: The Prison Letters of Justin Booth
Copyright © 2015 compiled and edited by Marcia Camp

Cowboy Buddha Publishing, LLC

No part of this book may be reproduced or transmitted in any form or by any means, electronic or mechanical, including photocopy, recording, or any information storage and retrieval system, without permission in writing from the author or his agents, except by a reviewer to be printed in a magazine or newspaper, or electronically transmitted on radio or television.

ISBN 978-0-9856076-3-0

Cover Photo by Mark McNabb
Author Photo by Angela Camp Dyke

Cover & Book Design by Jessica Dyer
Copy Editing by Scott Murphy
Illustrations by Justin Booth
Publishing Logo by Ted Nichols

March 2015

        Cowboy Buddha Publishing, LLC
              Benton, Arkansas

INTRODUCTION

This collection of letters started out to be a self-help book showing want-to-be poets that they could read the words of leading poets and prose writers and, along with Justin's take on them, be transformed into poets as he had been.

The author included the letters' dates for continuity, but chose to delete all salutations and closings so that readers could get right to their study of a poet's beginnings. However, after a well-known writer suggested that they be returned to the manuscript, I followed his advice, and they became the book's heart and soul. Instead of a how-to, it became a work detailing the relationship between a poet and the mentor who mailed material along with bits of her own poetry that had influenced him.

The thoughtful reader will experience the give-and-take of a poet's budding into the successful one he is today. Behind bars, his inquiring mind and eagerness to understand the prose and poetry he read and responded to led the fledgling writer to become a prize-winning poet.

Although I did everything I could to get Justin off the streets, I now realize that days on the street and nights spent sleeping on the sidewalk were absolutely necessary to his poetry. Never does he seem to be an observer, rather he is always the participant that he truly was and still is.

– Marcia Camp

FOREWORD

At the first meeting, Justin was dressed in his street clothes, yet he was clean and presentable. He was immediately able to join in discussion about various popular and/or famous poets in a comprehensive way. Of course, we were charmed, but I was struck by the desire it must have required to visit such a group without knowing what to expect.

The group actually included a farm wife, several college professors, a number of teachers, a nun, a woman who is an expert on horses and writes about them, and another woman who never graced a college campus.

Justin kept nervously glancing over his shoulder at the clock on the wall, and I knew he was timing his need for the next drink. I had never witnessed that kind of courage before.

This book illustrates the quality of poetry a caring, sharing, open-minded group can foster.

– Marcia Camp

I met Marcia the first time I went to a meeting of the River Market group of The Poets Roundtable Arkansas in Little Rock. Although I was still homeless and a drunken dope fiend, I had begun taking my work as a writer more seriously. I had seen a small blurb in the paper about the meeting and decided to go.

I arrived at the meeting at 10 in the morning on a Saturday very nervous about going two full hours without a drink – probably a little dope-sick. I expected to find beatniks with bongos and berets or maybe sexy co-eds dressed in black scribbling angst.

Instead, there was a half dozen older women, a sweet little man, also older, and a lady who wrote about horses. There was one attractive lady my age but she scared me most of all. I had gone a long time without talking to women. No sooner than I tried to back pedal out of there, Marcia took my hand and began talking to me in that aristocratic, Southern manner that she has, making it nearly impossible to escape. I kept coming back and Marcia became both a friend and a teacher. She remained so through rehabs and prisons.

Meeting her and the rest of the poets that day became instrumental in my developing any real technique as a poet and a writer. It was the letters that she and I exchanged in prison, with her editing my work and tirelessly researching, copying and sending me the works of greater men and women, that helped me to become the new and improved man I am now.

– Justin Booth

These letters were written by Justin Booth while he was serving time in the Grimes Unit near Newport, Arkansas, Pulaski County Jail and the Diagnostic Unit in Pine Bluff, Arkansas.

April 14, 2010

Dear Marcia,

I hope this finds you well. I have lots of time for my thoughts to run amok, and so I alternate between concern that you are unwell, and paranoid thoughts that you for some reason have decided against writing. I hope that neither turns out to be the case, that maybe we mis-communicated the address and so I write this letter.

I have been reading what I can, some books have been better than others. I had never read Shelley's *Frankenstein*, for example, and was surprised that I didn't really know the story. Mostly just pop fiction stuff — crime novels, etc.

I met a guy named _____ who says he is a screenwriter. While I am unsure if that is true (you hear some tall tales in here), he did have an appreciation and some insight into some poetry and authors that I enjoy, and we both talked for some time about literature until he was "shipped out" to federal prison for tax evasion.

I am still in the dark as to what will become of me, but cannot control that so I worry little about it. I have written a couple of poems and hope to write more, and I draw quite a bit. My hope is that I will be released soon, but I am trying to find a compromise of my former lifestyle and the all-controlling one I left behind on Broadway.

Some of the guys here have lived in various chem-free houses in the area, and I constantly pick them for information, hoping to find one that will suit my fancy. I admit now it was a mistake to have left the Serenity House.

In case you have tired of me, I will keep this short in order to not make an ass of myself but will include the poems nonetheless. (In truth, I cannot stand the thought of that, but have so little to say …) I hope the group, your family and you are all well.

Justin

[Editor's Note: Poems that have been published since these letters were written are not included in this book.]

April 14, 2010

Dear Marcia,

I got your note that you wrote on the 10th. I got the impression that you may have mailed a letter previously.

I have been waiting for the "packet" you said you were putting together with the Larry Brown information in it. I certainly was glad to hear from you anyway.

I have been reading the newspaper (a couple of days late) and I saw that *Oxford American* magazine honored a Little Rock author named Charles Portis, who wrote *True Grit*, and some other things. Not only did I not know we had such a highly esteemed author here, I didn't realize that the John Wayne film had started out as a novel. I look forward to reading Portis when I get out — *Dog of the South* sounds like an interesting read. I also wrote Harryette Mullen's name as someone I wanted to try and find at the library, but alas, I made no other notes about her and cannot remember why she was in the news.

I begin to be doubtful that I will in fact make it to court before the Spring Luncheon of the Poets' Roundtable of Arkansas, but if I miss it I know that there will be others to look forward to. I do hope it goes well and that the River Market Poets have a great time. I say that I doubt my court date is before then because others here have been set for the same judge as myself on the 28th of May. Certainly not the end of the world, I try to "keep my chin up" as you say.

I finally was able to trade my dessert for a stamped envelope, and got a letter in the mail this morning, then received yours at mail call this afternoon. Luckily we had cake again for dinner, so I hope this one lets you know that I do not mean to let you worry about me. I am afraid boredom is my biggest antagonist here, and the note you sent has me walking on the ceiling – I was overjoyed!

Oh, another thing — one of my neighbors told me about a place called Riverbend, in North Little Rock — not that different than Serenity Park. An initial program, followed by housing and a job. I intend to look into it — I still have hope for a semi-normal life, certainly I don't want to keep going to jail.

I normally don't write on the backs, but I am short on paper (and favors). I guess I have rambled on enough for now, so I'll close. I almost feel as if you have been right here with me talking — like we did sitting at your kitchen table. I have my share of difficulties, but I also have a wonderful friend in you. Thank you for that.

Justin

April 28, 2010

Marcia,

Wow, for the second time in the last week, an inmate has attempted to kill a jailer here. The latest one who was selected was really a good guy. I am shocked that anyone would try and harm him. I hear that his skull is fractured and that he is in bad shape at the hospital. Fortunately, I am doing well and able to stay clear, for the most part, of people like that.

I know I want to find some place that is "chem-free" and will accept me with no money to start with, but not so structured as to demand all of my time and deny me the opportunity to read and write. Maybe that is asking a little much, but it at least is an ideal I am shooting for.

The night is winding down, and silence begins to reign — such a wonderful absence of chaos. It is my favorite time of the day. Suddenly, my mind begins to stroll through hundreds of thoughts, memories, and imagined situations. I have been working on more serious poems, the ones that do not come together quickly but become more rewarding in the end.

While this is not the best environment for me, it is not the worst either. I have made some friends who have helped me out with paper and a pencil — though my pencil is on its last leg (about two inches long). I will put this letter away for now and write more tomorrow or the next day — Good Nite.

Oddly enough, I get newspapers, but only after they are a week old (or more), but I just read the story about the Zoo Poetry project. I was reminded of my very first River Market Poets meeting when we discussed it.

In another paper (March 30th), I read about a Fayetteville poet named Miller Williams turning 80 years old — I see that he did something at the Walton Arts Center last month. Could there be so many talented writers in Arkansas, and I just never noticed? I have started a list of local writers that I have been unaware of up until now. I will try and read them all when I have a chance. It's 2 a.m. and I am the only one here awake. I just thought I'd say "Hi," because the poetry stuff in the paper made me think of you. Will write more tomorrow.

I got your letter dated the 23rd — unfortunately not the first one. I am sorry I had no idea that they returned mail with envelopes enclosed. I would have thought they would have notified me some way at least. Anyway, it was wonderful to hear from you and know that I am in your thoughts. I cannot relay to you how good it is for my morale to know I have friends. Knowing that letters were sent, even though I didn't get them makes me feel good. I have begun to sell off more of my trays, I am tired of most of the entrées anyway, but I have fixed myself with materials with which I can correspond.

By the time you get this, the Spring Luncheon will be complete — let me know how it went. I will wait eagerly to hear from you, for now I will close.

Justin

April 30, 2010

Dear Marcia,

I am concerned about these disturbing phone calls that you got. I hope that they are a thing of the past. I really can't imagine that their origins have to do with the mail here, but given a choice between you suffering any sort of harassment and me getting mail, I would forgo a letter in a moment. Please be careful and don't allow my situation to give you any discomfort.

I have had the most wonderful day, having received two different letters from you! The lady from the mail room came down to tell me that I couldn't receive stamped envelopes. She brought a letter dated the 21st and allowed me to keep it but said she would have to dispose of the offending envelope (a bargain).

I will not allow such an important regulation to spoil the unbridled happiness that erupted in me upon receiving your correspondence. I was so happy that I shared your correspondence with a friend named _____, a name that I am sure means little to you, but you may well know his Aunt _____ who works at the library downtown.

As far as my ability to draw goes, it may surprise you to know that my earliest ambition (like around the time I was 8 or 9 years old) was to be a cartoonist. Alas, it may well cost me any hope I may have of ever being a serious student of art, as I had developed a stylized way of drawing that I never could quite escape, and was fairly run out of high school art class on a rail. I still sometimes consider buying a simple "starter kit" of paints, thinking that it would be a hobby I would enjoy even though, in truth, I have never painted anything other than a house!

Justin

May 5, 2010

Dear Marcia,

How are you my friend? I am fine. I got your latest letter (4-29) and was pleased as always to hear from you! I was amused at your description of your work/eating schedule.

I was telling a friend the other day about the time I spent with you before going to rehab — almost all of it in your kitchen! Food and talk go together so much better than food and research.

My friends in here are not the most literate folks and they seemed to enjoy the "rhyming poems" I wrote. I have started selling them for an envelope each! So far, three Mother's Day, and one "for my girl" poem. I hope they lose them before my fame is established. HA! I also wrote a letter for a fellow to send to his judge — I don't know if it will help, but I get paid for the writing not the results. The poems make greeting cards seem works of art, but if I sold out, it was for a good cause.

The gallery in the research library *[The Butler Center for Arkansas Studies]* is one of my favorite places. I go, sometimes more than once, to enjoy each show. I look forward to seeing the exhibit that you wrote about. When the gallery first opened, they had a collection of old black-and-white photographs, portraits mostly, all taken in Arkansas prisons.

I have been racking my brain about Miller Williams — I would have sworn that Maya Angelou was the poet who read at Clinton's inauguration. *[Both of these poets wrote and read their inaugural poems.]* I was quite active at that time in volunteering. I was in college at Arkansas State University in Jonesboro and came to Little Rock for his speech when he won. I do tend get things muddled in my mind though. Please try and send one of his poems in with your next letter — my curiosity is overwhelming.

I am sending you another poem, more in my usual style. I hope you find it interesting. I will close now and return to *East of Eden*, as the lights have gone low, and the others are sleeping. I cannot believe that I was able to get this book — can you believe no one wanted it? And it had lain idle for quite a while! It is so beautifully written I often laugh out loud, only to find myself deeply saddened moments later. Anyway, I run on —

        Signed your dysfunctional friend,
                    Justin

May 7, 2010

Dear Marcia,

So happy to hear from you. Not much change in here. I finished the Steinbeck novel, though I had to go to the library to check out a copy to actually finish.

The barter system is alive and well here, men trade items off their trays for other items, or entire meals (such as tonight's dinner for tomorrow's breakfast). Sometimes commissary items for tray items; and of course services like the letters I told you about writing or maybe doing the clean-up chore for someone. It is a game of a kind that tickles me when I sit back and watch for the details.

There has been some tension lately as the crowding becomes a problem, and people wait for months longer than they should before leaving for the penitentiary. Believe it or not the "time" is better there than here. There, you have a job and activities where here is sort of "human warehousing," with only a minimum of things to look forward to. In my case, mail call is the highlight of the day, and yesterday I received a letter from you, making me feel quite special.

I am amazed at your amount of saved resources and cannot even begin to fathom what the time must have been like for the dissident from Russia. Your poem in her honor was touching. Surely more so to those of us who write because we have to. I would imagine that she would have been punished for even scratching words in soap.

Irina Ratushinskaya (by Marcia Camp)

Humbly I write on clean, moored paper
of you who etched poems in soap
cleansed your soul
of words that took flight,
though prison bars held your body fast,
lungs decaying in dank cell,
you memorized the scratched-out words
then sent them in tiny bubbles
to oblivion—
two-hundred-fifty poems.
Free now, you remember every line—
each bar of soap your tenuous hold
on sanity—
each poem your claim
to immortality.

I hate that I missed the Luncheon. Sorry the Board stuff tainted your experience. I wish people would recognize how much you care about poetry and trust you as I do.

"Some Things in Life" is a brave leap into vulnerability. It has power. I know it may seem odd to you that I mention it just now, but it is that kind of power I know, full of vulnerability, that makes you so right for the position.

I have run out of paper, so I guess I will get this in the mail. Goodness knows I miss you and can't wait to see you again.

                        Justin

May 14, 2010

Dear Marcia,

I got your letter and the poems you sent; feel a little goofy because you gave me a copy of "Let Me Tell You" by Miller Williams once at your house, I forgot who wrote it, I guess. It was the one he wrote for his children that moved me the most. I have a son and two daughters myself. I think if I were to die, I would want someone to read it at my funeral. A morbid thought, to be sure, but I will make copies and send them to family members with instructions just in case.

I have been remiss in writing because I have been working on something in the pattern that Williams wrote that poem — ABA repeated five times then ABAA — it is difficult and so far not so good, but I enjoy it like some people enjoy those number puzzles, Sudoku.

After *East of Eden*, I found I was in no particular hurry to start another book, preferring instead to just think about the power of Steinbeck's description and theme. The night I finished, I laid awake hours both pleased and envious.

Oh, back to the "Hard Times" poem you wrote — I have always thought that vulnerability was absolutely essential in writing in order for the reader to empathize — I certainly don't see it as a weakness. I do not consider you wimpy! More like "laying bare your soul" that you talk about in the "Fear and Loathing" essay from April/May/June 1998.

I am intrigued by the essays on homelessness that you judged, so few people really understand much at all about it because the homeless themselves are so varied in type and situation.

Some Things in Life (by Marcia Camp)

have been hard,
childbirth comes to mind,
closing my father's spent blue eyes
for that last long sleep,
having to make love when
I felt only hate,
but the hardest was
when my child, lying gray
against hospital-white sheets,
asked me to sing.

I have a couple of friends who "share" some of the things you write and send. They saw your photo beside your byline and were talking about how attractive you are. Of course, I egged them on — told them you were a redhead etc. They were having a tough time with the concept of a friendship like ours or at least were teasing me about it. It was all in good fun (and good taste).

I'll go for now, bye, your pen pal,
Justin

May 18, 2010

Dear Marcia,

Hi, how are you doing? I am okay, getting a little stir crazy, but making it.

I got your note today but none of the stuff you sent along so it looks like I'll have to wait a little longer to look that material over. I spoke with the women from the mail room here, it is photocopied newspaper articles and photographs that are considered contraband. That is why I got the poetry and essays but not the other things. Anyway, I have been trying to "hustle" a book but no luck so far.

I have been kicking a plot line around in my head for a full-length book. I'm guessing 100,000 words would be a low-ball guess on "full length." ... Oddly, just thinking about it has helped to pass time.

I miss writing stories, I did more of it in the past, only recently has my focus been on poetry. It is the not-knowing what is going on that is giving me troubles, I haven't even received anything that tells me that I am going to court and when that will be, so I am trying to adjust to the idea that it may be a little longer. Oh, well.

I don't have much more room, but tomorrow the "store" runs, I have made some barter for more paper and a couple of envelopes, so will close for now. Just wanted to "chat" for a moment. I am thankful to have such a good friend.

                Until I see you again,
                Justin

June 2, 2010

Dear Marcia,

What a wonderful letter I got from you yesterday! I am happy that your presentation went well for you, but I never had a single doubt that it would.

As far as my situation and attitude — it is easy for me to remain upbeat knowing that you (and members of River Market Poets) are thinking of me and hoping for the best. I cannot express in words the value that I place on these friendships and my association with others who love the written word as much as I do.

Please do not concern yourself overly with my safety. The "rules" of this "society" are, as you would guess, based on the Law of the Jungle — the strongest live better than everyone else. What you may not have guessed is that intellectual strength often has more clout than physical strength. While I may not be the smartest guy, I am, say, at the meeting of writers from around the state, in this place I am highly respected and my advice is considered of worth.

It will be more so in prison. Many of these men, no matter how imposing, are really frightened. They live in the darkness of ignorance. I purposely work on giving them reassurance, making allies of as many of them as possible. It is complex, it is its own little world, but one that I can do well enough in. I have begun framing a short story about this world in my mind.

Actually, at this point more about setting — the power classes, racial tensions, etc. — than the plot I want them "read" in. I am quite caught up in the details of it, so maybe I will find an audience for it.

I also have been writing a "relationship" story about two street people who try and re-enter "normal" society. The plot involves a lottery ticket they hope will be a "winner."

In the end, the ticket won't be, but they see that they are (winners). I have a little over 3,000 words and it will probably double that in the end.

I wonder if this (20 pages) seems long, short or average for a short story. I suppose it depends on the magazine that would want stories, but my experience has been reading collected short stories by well-known authors, and I am sure the number of pages/words were quite varied.

Now I wanted to thank you for the Ginsberg poetry. It was the nicest gift you could send me. "3456 W. 15th St." was one of the first poems by him that I ever read. It is a wonderful poem. Written in couplets with broken space lines — I like the song-like quality of meter in combination with gritty subject. It is the kind of poem I wish I could write. I read and re-read all three of them all night. I am sure I'll read them one-thousand more times before I leave. Thank you, thank you, thank you.

I have begun (like I said) to work at some prose, so I knew I'd need a great deal more (paper). I think that I should be able to glean a story or two from this experience. Please keep me in your mind as you will be in mine.

Love ya,
Justin

June 17, 2010

Dear Marcia,

How are you, my friend, I am fine, it is Saturday night, and I was sitting here a little bored so I thought I'd start a letter. Maybe only a few lines for now, but it always helps me to relax.

Things are pretty much the same day-for-day here, but I do have a new roommate. His name is _____, and he is from Chihuahua, Mexico. I have been learning a little Spanish from him, and some of it is even acceptable in polite conversation. Simple stuff really, fundamental to have, like the names of suits of playing cards, for example. He saw me writing and asked what it was, you should've seen the time I had explaining what a poem was.

I had no frame of reference, and couldn't think of a single Mexican writer. Finally, I read him one of the elementary love poems I'd written, and I suppose he recognized meter and rhyme and a huge smile broke out on his face. The funniest part is the word for poem in Spanish is "poema" but our dialects and accents are so different that it took us awhile. He is a good example of the complexity of some of the people here. He was in prison in Mexico a while back for stabbing a man, and there was a pistol involved in his arrest this time (I haven't gleaned the details), but he is good natured, friendly and always smiling. I rather enjoy his company, and we spend a great deal of our time sharing our respective languages with each other. You can tell, I suppose.

Could you possibly know how much it means to me to get your letters? Then today, I got two at once. Sooo very happy! Thank you for sending the rather lengthy, "Howl" by Allen Ginsberg. I believe it was only the first of the three sections that I had read before. I admired him because his subject matter seems to be similar to what I want to share, but he does it without seeming trite or like he is trying to "shock" the reader in a way that is cheap.

I have been working with _____ on his English some. Certainly, he speaks enough to get by — but he can hardly read in English. Our vowels change sounds and this among other things confuses him, and he would like to make his accent more American.

I read poetry to him and then read with him, coaching, as he repeats it back to me. It has been good for both of us I think. Some nights he reads from whatever paperback I happen to have around. It is painstaking but rewarding.

I find myself looking forward to prison where restrictions on what materials I can receive will be lessened, as well as a few other benefits of a living environment. If nothing else, it is the next phase of my journey, and I know I must go there in order to return here and see you and all the others I've begun to think of as friends.

I will close because I'd like to share some new poems.

Justin

June 24, 2010

Dear Marcia,

So nice to get the Kerouac stuff from you. The intro/biography that you included, describing how Ed White suggested that Kerouac "sketched in the streets like a painter but with words." Wow! That blew me away, I have never heard it put that way, but sort of in my own way, it is what I aspire to do. Jail here is very limiting to stimuli, in a way arresting to the senses. So bland and boring in its repetitiveness. Prison, however, will be so much more colorful. I expect I will take notes constantly and draw on the experience for years to come. The "brief look through the doorway" that you described to me before, I hope will be my last, but I will use it and share its story with others.

Did I mention my contraband desk made from stolen (from the trash) cardboard that I have covered in old newspapers I have glued on with toothpaste? It makes writing so much easier, though it is difficult for me to hide during "shakedowns."

I am glad you liked the last two poems I sent, I'm partial to "Where We All Sleep" myself. Do you write something and it seems a little above your other efforts to your own way of thinking? That one sort of did, to me. I have my original draft of "The Poetry of Night," but I made several (three more) drafts of "Where …" and, I went back to re-read it couldn't find the earlier versions. I have a neighbor who sent one of those home to someone (how he got it I'm not sure). I'm friendly with him, but I think he stole my writing, and I am quietly angry about it.

I am pleased at your suggestion/offer to assist me in entering some contests. I looked over the list and believe (there are several) that I easily qualify to enter. I am the luckiest guy here, because, with your help, the things I love most remain fairly uninterrupted.

I got your second letter (this week) and more from sketches. How funny, I could picture your reaction to the typewriter problem. I feel much the same way about writing as you do, and a good deal of my time is spent gathering materials.

                      Thank you,
                      Justin

June 30, 2010

Dear Marcia,

I am pleased to hear that you may be at the close in the sale of the "Great Lawn Decoration" *[a 30-foot motor home]*. I assume that by now one or the other interested parties has actually taken delivery of the behemoth.

I will jump right to the subject of the contest, if you don't mind, as I have couple of questions.

1) What is the cut-off date for entry?
2) Contest No. 10 says Form Sonnet — would you remind me exactly of the rhyming scheme/syllables per line?

Oddly enough when you first sent the list to me, I put check marks by contests, and when you sent the last letter, the "recommended" group you listed was nearly identical.

I have a couple of envelopes coming, but for now only one and I am anxious to get these poems to you.

Justin
Genus Irritable Vatum
(The Irritable Tribe of Poets)

July 7, 2010

Dear Marcia

I forgot to mention in my last letter that I saw a story in the newspaper about a Marvel Comics artist who lives in Little Rock with his wife. It surely is the guy you mentioned in a previous letter.

It has cooled off some, and I am happy for that. I spend more and more time outdoors here. I grow tired of this place and these people, and find myself looking for ways to "escape" into myself. In the last week or so, there has been quite a turnover, with many of the people I was closest to leaving for home, prison, or just another unit here. Change seems more shocking here I suppose since so little ever changes for the good. I survive however, and I look forward to leaving myself and moving on to the next step.

I can't think of a single ghost story that I could reference in some tangible way. I tried to think about any Arkansas prison ghosts but can't think of any specific examples. Then I saw an old postcard in the Style section of the *Arkansas Democrat-Gazette* that featured a photograph of "Old Sparky," the electric chair that was used, and I also thought of the shallow graves of deceased convicts they discovered after the prison reformation in the '60s I think but again, no "specific" ghosts.

I don't know (and I am sure the competition for the $1,000 will be tough) but I'd like to try anyway.

Okay, I took a little break. It's now Saturday night. I have been thinking about the Arkansas ghost poem quite a bit. How extensive a bibliography do they want? What form is that supposed to take? Proving your research for art seems peculiar to me, but

I am intrigued by the topic as well as the potential prize money. I'm sure I'm only repeating myself at this point, but it is pretty much all I have thought of the last week or so.

Well, I was the just the receiver of a cell "shakedown." My cardboard desk went untouched, however, they took my extra bed sheet and my six or seven small packets of salt and pepper. I managed to get the salt and pepper back when the guard wasn't looking, but no luck with the sheet. I don't mind. It makes them so happy to find contraband occasionally, I keep my desk and let them get the small stuff.

I am sending a couple of poems, along with the caption that was under the postcard – you'll notice an address:

Little Rock, circa 1926, The new electric chair at the state prison in Little Rock is shown here. Gov. Junius M. Futrell closed the facility in 1933, all inmates were moved to the Cummins and Tucker Farms. The death chamber was moved to Tucker. The method of execution had been changed from hanging to the electric chair in 1913. Constructed of wood taken from the dismantled state gallows, "Old Sparky" as it was nicknamed, was used in 104 executions between 1926 and 1948. In the early years, the executioner stood next to the condemned man when operating the instrument of death.

From: Arkansas Postcard Past
by Steve Hanley
The Arkansas Democrat-Gazette
June 26, 1910

[Victims' family members were invited to attend electrocutions. The amount of electricity and intensity was at the discretion of the executioner. This form of "justice" could easily become torture.]

I wonder if I wrote the Hanley guy, if he might send me any more information about the electric chair. What do you think?

I think I will close now, as I am dog tired. I will write again soon, for one thing I am betting that I get a letter from you before you get this one. Know that you're on my mind as well as the other poets.

                With loving friendship,
                      Justin

July 12, 2010

Dear Marcia,

Hi! How are you doing? I hope you're well and had a great holiday.

I'm sending some poems for contests and hoping that you can read my writing. *[These poems have not been included in this book because several have already been published in Justin's* "Trailer Park Troubadour: Strung Out On Heartbreak," *2013.]*

I don't know how many poems I have actually sent, I should have written down the particulars, but alas, I did not. Read "dumb and lazy." I hope you'll do me the additional favor of picking the ones you think are best. I know you are trying to do many other things, and I really appreciate your doing this for me.

My friend from Mexico was supposed to be released yesterday but has a hold on him from Immigration *[and Naturalization Services]*. They will take him back to Mexico. It wasn't in his plans really, but I can tell he is pleased when he talks about seeing his mother and brother and sisters, so I guess everything will be for the best.

I was looking at some paperwork and it seems I haven't been waiting for my next stop as long as I thought, so I'll probably be here close to a month yet. I don't get mail on Saturdays, but I am betting I hear from you Monday. The absolute highlight of my week!

With fond thoughts,
Justin

July 13, 2010

Dear Marcia,

I got your letter and am on fire to get started on my "ghost" poem. It is a wonderful thing to be onto something that fills my days in such a wonderful way. I honestly don't have enough time some days to get everything done that I would like to.

Before I forget, could we shift gears from poetry you've been sending me (and saving my life) to at least some of the work done by Donald Harington. *[I furnished the unpublished manuscript by Bernie Babcock from which Harington wrote* The Choiring of the Trees *in 1991, about convict Neal McLaughlin.]* Also, I'd like to take you up on the offer to write Steve Hanley for me as well.

The uncertainty of when I'll move is the only constant in my life within these walls, but a person who was sentenced three weeks before I was left this morning so that is indicative (at least to me) that I will be leaving in about that much more time. The first place I'll go is called "diagnostics," and it will be about 10 days or so of isolation. I think that will be a good place to write, a lot of people tell me how boring that portion is. After that, 60 days of "hoe squad" or hard labor. I worry that I will be too tired to write then, but we will have weekends off, so there is that. Of course in my fantasies, I will win some contest money and have that to help in re-starting my life upon my release. My mind reels with possibilities, when I allow it to. I will undoubtedly parole out to a "halfway house," and I plan to start off in a positive way, working, writing, and living indoors. I would gladly take restaurant work or whatever, so long as I can be self-supporting and still have time to write.

I will close now and set my mind to Ginsberg before making

a few notes tonight in the way of possible "plots" for my ghost poem.

                Thanks a million,
                Justin

July 16, 2010

Dear Marcia,

Thanks for the Bukowski stuff. I love "So You Want to Be a Writer." I mentioned it the first day I ever met you. I was talking about the lines where he says:

> "If you first have to read it to your wife
> or your girlfriend or your boyfriend
> or parents or to anybody at all,
> you're not ready."

Of course, I do love sharing my poetry with you, but I understand the difference now. I write because I write — but I share it because I choose to.

I have been exercising for about two hours a day for the last two weeks. I started so that I wouldn't be in such poor shape when I hit the "hoe squad" portion of my time, but even in the short time I can see a noticeable difference in the size and shape of my arms. Pleasing to my middle-aged vanity.

I wrote the enclosed "Joella ..." poem — I hope it's not too shocking. I don't see it in any contest, but it just came out. *[This poem was published in Justin's most recent book,* The Singer, The Lesbian & The One With The Feet, *2015]*

I am sure that my neighbors have decided that I am quite insane. Crazy, it seems, for your poem "Onions." I have read it aloud so many times – it is such a moving poem, deceptive in its simplicity, sharing a peek into three generations and their humaneness.

If I have been your coffee break without coffee, then you are my parole without exodus. I can't say enough times how much all you're doing means to me. It has been my medicine in the sickest of places. I yearn to chat and laugh with you and look forward to that day.

                                            Justin

Onions (by Marcia Camp)

make me cry — not the
lush purple Italians or sweet Vidalias —
slim, willowy ones, scallions up North,
but below the Mason-Dixon, green onions.

They're hardy — a must for any kitchen garden,
a must for someone who tills the soil
to know he's yet a man — still needed,
still defined by useful work
as my father was those final years.

In my backyard, he found a tiny sunny spot,
planted sets from his cousin's truck patch.
He weeded and loosened the soil
with a two-pronged cooking fork.

His onions cling to life now,
two summers since he left them —
tough, misshapen from their struggle,
nodding green tops heavy with sets.

Now my son is home, wounded by life and love.
He told a friend, "I'm back in the room
I had in high school, and
everything I own is in there with me."

He finds tiny sunny spot, breaks ground,
turning over mounds of tradition,
looking for his roots.
Bending broad shoulders,
thrusting forward a slightly graying head,

he will place each heirloom set with care.

As I watch his shovel search for the courage
of his forebears, see him try to unearth
a reason to go on,
onions make me cry.

Ode to Bacon (by Marcia Camp)

Today I feel the need to fry bacon,
let its renderings' smokey musk fill every room.
Someone said, "If you're moving to the South,
start saving your bacon grease —
they'll tell you what to do with it."

But we won't — can't — there are no words,
only symbols that remind us that
we fought and lost a war on our own soil;
lost our men in their thousands,
some broken men returned with
empty sleeves and trouser legs; then we felt
the cruel heel of reconstruction on our necks.

For four long years those at home starved,
yet a few drops of that magic potion transformed
wild greens and field peas into ambrosia,
became common ethnic food that bound blacks
      and whites.
It was the elixir of courage,
its scent worn like an amulet.

It has become each person's patinaed bronze
      soldier,
horse rearing on courthouse lawn;
our own Scarlett clutching a turnip, black
      earth clinging,
while against a red sky, Atlanta burns;
still so precious that a southern woman,
making that final journey to daughter's house or
      nursing home,
offers her Mason jar of bacon drippings
to a friend or loved one.

No, we will not tell them…
cannot tell them … for words fail to plumb
the reasons why on this day
I feel the need to fry bacon.

[Historians recently revised the number of Civil War casualties, adjusting the total from 650,000 to 800,000.]

July 26, 2010

Marcia,

I will just write a quick note. A guy who was sentenced the same time as me left two days ago, and they generally go in order. I think that I will be able to keep all my writings, but given the nature of this poem, I wanted to go ahead and send it. It is of course, my entry, so there you go. I have taken at least a thousand dollars worth of pleasure in its creation, so I have already won. Please let me know what you think of it when you can.

— If I leave next week, I'll send a letter with my new address as soon as I can. Could you please help with the reference page? I don't know what they want, as I have never done one.

                                        Justin

July 27, 2010

Dear Marcia,

I am doing well and hope you are as well. I feel confident I will be transferred to what is called the Diagnostic Unit in Pine Bluff this week. I cannot know for sure because of security reasons, but in case I cannot take an envelope with me, I am sending what will be my next address:

>Dean Booth 654438
>Diagnostic Unit
>8707 W. Seventh
>Pine Bluff, AR 71601

I will try and write from there as soon as I can. I, of course, am a little in the dark, but I have been told that due to overcrowding, I may be at home as early as October. Wouldn't it be wonderful if I could attend Poetry Day with everyone? Will it be in Little Rock again? Not that it matters, but it would be such a nice coming-home gift of fate. I am writing this hurriedly so I will be sure it gets out — so not much of a letter, but I want to be sure my pen pal knows where I am.

>Justin

August 2, 2010

Dear Marcia,

Well, it's Sunday evening. I have my fingers crossed again for next week. I feel so good about getting this out of the way that I am downright giddy. It's not, of course, that I am so excited about prison, but it is the next step to coming home and being with all of you and taking another stab at returning to a more normal lifestyle.

I imagine myself, this time, doing a much better job of it.

If I go to work fairly quickly, and I am sure I will, I will try and buy a laptop or other device to make things easier for my writing.

I feel confident that I will live in some sort of transitional living facility, and it wouldn't take much of a job for me to be able to swing it.

I lie awake at night sometimes and think of what it would be like to read at the Spring Luncheon — God, what an ego! I told you that there is a chance, though slim, that I would be out by October, didn't I?

It seems that every three months the "system" does what is called an Emergency Powers Act kick out. It is possible I would be on that list in September, as I would be "short" by then anyway. The variables are unending, so it is nearly impossible to compute, but I will have a good idea next week when I actually enter the "system."

I am enjoying a special treat tonight, instant Maxwell House coffee, a friend was able to get it and shared a few cups (spoonfuls) with me. So I feel a little bit free.

Please don't be overly concerned about "hoe squad" — I am actually looking forward to the experience for a myriad of reasons. It will be a good workout, I will tan, and I am sure it will be one of those wonderful "peeks through a door" that will lend itself to my writing.

Thanks for the new Bukowski stuff, I really love him for what he can do in so few words. I admire him but have to concentrate that I don't "copy" his style, especially since our experiences seem so similar in so many ways. I don't want to be a "knock off" of him, but I do want some of that "magic" and "honesty" that he so readily exhibits in his work.

I so look forward to wearing nice clothes. We wear uniforms that are torn, dirty, and ill-fitting. You and I both know I don't dress nice every day, but it is one the main things I miss.

Justin

August 4, 2010

Dear Marcia,

I am officially moved to Pine Bluff. It has been fun so far. They woke me up at about 3:30 in the morning and told me I was leaving. I grabbed my letters and things and went and put on my civilian clothes and waited. Got on a bus and waited. Drove 45 minutes and came inside — looked at, TB test, medical screen, and now I'm in a bullpen and waiting some more again. Forgive my handwriting, I have a flexible ink pen designed to be an ineffective weapon, unfortunately a side-effect is that is also an ineffective writing implement.

I'm finally given a cell, and lucky me, I am placed next to the two loudest people in the entire Arkansas Department of Corrections. We, at least this barracks, are housed in one-man cells. Locked down 23 hours a day. I cannot discern a pattern to how and when things are done, so I'll just keep watching.

Seems complex, but I know you can handle it. I am totally exhausted, and I think they just called "Shower Call." So I won't worry trying too hard to fill the page, instead I will take my hygiene and then sit back and go over my inmate handbook, then maybe grab a few ZZZs.

Oh, one more thing. I will only be here about three weeks then I'll go to where I'll finish things off. Time-wise, I don't know yet where that final place will be, but will keep you informed.

      Wish I were there,
      Justin

August 7, 2010

Marcia,

I am up reading and realize that tomorrow is Sunday — so no mail will go out. I may as well write anyhow.

The food is much better here — at the very least there is more of it. However, you've not much time to eat. When all the rows (there aren't many) of tables fill up, the first row must stand up and leave. Maybe three or four minutes to eat. I do well because it is similar to basic training and I remember to eat on my way to the table and again on my way to put my tray up. There's that good ol' Army training paying off, eh?

It is quiet, finally, here and cooler. I'm more happy during this time of solitude than any other time, regardless of where I am. It just seems mystical somehow, and my thoughts run like wild dogs in tall grass flushing rabbits that won't be caught, quite, before another jumps up.

My next-door neighbor has just quit talking in the last hour or so. He was sentenced to 70 years "on the yoke," which means as a Y Class felony, he'll do 70 percent of 70 years. He is 37. He won't meet Old Sparky, but he'll die in prison nonetheless. I don't know why I mention it, I've just had it on my mind.

There are more of the same "children" here as in Pulaski, — 18-, 19-, and 20-year-olds make up the bulk of people going to prison it would seem. They speak with forced bravado, making joking references to homosexual rape. I can tell they are frightened. The truth is that it is something that probably won't happen. An endless cycle of out-again/in again should scare them more. It's a very a real possibility for most of them. Gosh, I'm somber.

I feel a poem coming on.

> Good night and God bless,
> Justin

August 7, 2010

Dearest Marcia,

I got my first letter today, and I couldn't believe the turnaround time. You could never know how wonderful it was — of course I knew it was coming, but I am all alone here, surrounded by hundreds of foul-mouthed, loud, abrasive personalities, and it was so good to just see the envelope with my address typed on the front.

I cannot be sure what all the specifics are yet, but I do know this:

- * Photos are allowed
- * Stamps, envelopes NOT allowed
- * Books, magazines, etc., are allowed so long as they are sent from the bookstore
- * Pretty sure the printed material you've been sending is okay, but can't find a reference in the handbook.

This place is sort of a hold/routing station, three tiers of 16 cells in my barracks. Kind of looks like the Elvis "Jailhouse Rock" movie set. The doors are bars, and the sink-toilet combo is one-piece stainless steel. We wear white jumpsuits/coveralls and blue slip-on "deck shoes." I should be here about another week or two, and then to my "primary unit." So long as you continue to address the mail the way you did on this one, it will "find" me, and I can update the address upon landing at the new place.

Glad you found the end of "Haunted," thanks for helping with the reference page. Thanks for all the typing and everything else.

Justin

August 16, 2010

Dear Marcia,

I have been spending my days reading, some stuff better than others. Right now, something called the *Nick Tosches Reader*. I never heard of the guy, but I find it an interesting read. Some poetry, some short short prose, reviews of albums (I'm guessing that is how he earned the biggest part of his income). He is a New Yorker, from W. 42nd, but apparently loves country music, lived in Nashville for a while, and wrote a book about it. It's pretty evident to me that he considers himself foremost a poet (his stuff is not the greatest, mostly shock-value stuff), but his commentary on good poets and poetry I find utterly compelling. Also some great quotes:

> "I have tried to write Paradise
> Let the wind speak/that is Paradise,"
> – Ezra Pound

He mentioned a poet named Charles Olson and includes some lines of his. I wonder, do you know his work? His free verse form is tall and skinny — two, three, maybe four words per line. Olson describes them as "breath lines" and emphasizes meter as the most important thing in poetry. "He who controls meter, controls everything." *[These tall, skinny "breath lines" ultimately became Justin's writing style.]*

Just got your letter and the typed copy of "Haunted." Boy, I am happy with that. Thanks so much for putting the effort in typing and doing the Bib., not to mention paying my dues and fees. You're a far better friend than I deserve, but please don't stop on account of that.

Oh, and if the Old Sparky/Statehouse exhibit runs until March 2011, I will make a point of seeing it.

Am enclosing another poem I wrote. Looks like my pen is dying so I'll close.

        Always grateful for your friendship,
                    Justin

Date Unknown

Dear Marcia,

I have been reading *The Artificial Southerner* by Philip Martin. It includes stories about Miller and Lucinda Williams, Johnny Cash among others, and what it means to be Southern. I feel sure you must know Mr. Martin. I so have enjoyed his book. If I have done nothing else during this time, I have become more familiar with Arkansas' writers and developed a sense of pride in the literature, poetry, and observations that come out of our geographical area. One other person mentioned in the book, or how 'bout two, are Larry Brown and Barry Hannah.

I read Barry Hannah for the first time some years ago. I was in a similar situation then. I was locked up for about a year in county jail, and a professor of English from Arkansas State University sent me a packet of books — I admit I had forgotten his name but was quick to remember his very Mississippi writing style upon reading his name. You know, I've read a couple of different authors, in interviews, who try to distance themselves from the handle of "Southern writer" — I wonder why that is. Could it be that no one wants to live in the shadow cast by Faulkner?

Justin

August 20, 2010

Dear Marcia,

How's my favorite pen pal? I got a letter today, and I am always amazed at how much hearing from you improves my mood. I have been singing and dancing around in my little one-man cell all afternoon.

My next-door neighbor here writes poetry. He beat a man to death with a hammer and will spend the next 55 years in prison on a 70-year sentence. His poetry is dark, and a little heavy handed at times but chilling and insightful at others. We talk sometimes for an hour standing at our cell doors. We cannot see each other, but we can easily hear each other without disturbing others. I have never asked him what compelled him to commit such an act (it is an unacceptable social faux pas here), but he is a small sensitive type and I cannot help but wonder about it.

According to the talk around here (and it seems amazingly accurate), most of us will be gone next week to our "regular" units. The "hoe squad" period is about to begin.

I wish I could convey to you how very important a part you have played in making this experience a positive one.

                    Thank you as always,
                    Justin

August 23, 2010

Dear Marcia,

I got a letter telling me my parole hearing would be October, so I'll miss Poetry Day, but just barely. I mentioned once before to you about the Maple Street House, I still have their address and will write them a letter soon in order to get my ducks in a row. I will have to file what is known as a parole plan, essentially stating where I intend to live. The sooner I can get it approved, the better.

I sit and fantasize sometimes about mundane things I would be doing if I were not here. Another advantage of an active imagination. It is never the "really big" things but rather the everyday ones I think of. The cool sensation of artificially chilled air as I pass through the inner doors of the library, or the Clinton School Gallery with its endless displays, or something (although this one is a stretch) working a simple job as a busboy/dishwasher so I can have plenty of time to read and write. I will do so now, I suppose, as I am short of paper.

I have copies of all the poems entered in the contests. Once more I want to thank you for all of your efforts, from editing, to typing, to actually footing the bill for fees and dues. I could not have done this without you. It has done wonders for me. Keeping me busy, giving me hope, and broadening my scope of subjects in my poetry. Really, I can't thank you enough. Please know how much I value you and your friendship.

                                    Justin

August 28, 2010

Dear Marcia,

I got your letter, it was like Manna. Is it not nearly as bad as you might think. I went out to a huge vegetable garden and picked okra all day with fat cowboys toting pistols riding between sections of different vegetables. It wasn't bad, in fact, if you put the horses and pistols out of your mind, kind of pleasant. On weekends, they show movies, this weekend some John Wayne flicks, some sort of fantasy, and an endearing movie about a girl with cancer and her sister (genetically engineered as a "donor child") who sues her parents for the rights to her own body.

I was able to finally visit a library, and though it was limited, I was so lucky. I got a copy of a book called *The Road* by Cormac McCarthy. I was reminded again of our conversations at your table, one of the books we talked about was *No Country For Old Men*. In this book that I am reading now, his use of language is a thing of beauty.

> "The blackness he woke to on those nights was sightless and impenetrable. A blackness to hurt your ears with listening."

That's so wonderfully said. He truly is a genius. Of course not so that I didn't set him aside to enjoy the short story you intended to send to "Grandmother Earth." Could not read it without hearing your voice every time the Southern girl talked. Good stuff, really.

I haven't written anything in a while, but have been getting snatches of ideas and phrases as I soak in my new living arrangements. Just trying to get used to everything for now.

A little excitement around here, someone must have smoked a cigarette — they have come on strong — searching some guys, whatever, none of my business.

Can't really think of much more to say for now, except that I miss you and all the others from River Market Poets. I guess I'll let you go for this one, get it in the mail.

                Thinking about you,
                Justin

September 3, 2010

Dear Marcia,

Got another letter, with the essay from the newspaper. I could hardly get it unfolded before _____ grabbed it, wanting to read it. You have a fanatic follower — he insists I tell you how much he enjoys your writing and has asked if I will mail you his poem when he finishes for your approval/comments. He tickles me, he doesn't have the greatest command of the English language, but he has a fairly sharp mind nonetheless. Just when I make a value judgment of his intelligence based on his limited vocabulary, he sees some reasonably subtle meaning in a line of poetry that he has read. Amazing.

I am waiting to watch *Alice in Wonderland,* the latest Johnny Depp film, such a macho prison movie, huh? It is nice that they show movies on weekends, some are better than others, most though, are PG. I can only guess why they started doing that. Tomorrow, *Where the Wild Things Are* — both were books I read to my children, and I am feeling nostalgic about them.

I am sharing some of your stuff with a guy named J.R. He really enjoyed the short story but was eager to have more. I have really gotten a kick out of him taking your characters and running with them. He reads all the poetry I have from my stuff to the best stuff of other Little Rock poets and keeps saying (with a huge smile on his face), "It doesn't even hafta rhyme, does it?"

Oh, and speaking of things that pleased me, I found it quite complimentary when you said you liked my poetry more than Bukowski's, but when you inferred that your own writing had been influenced in some way (more gritty) by my own — it was the highest praise I have ever received.

Also, I can't recall if I ever commented on the "Prozac" poem by Christine Delea. I hope that she goes on to write more humorous stuff, and I get to read it. That was so funny.

You asked to mention other poets that I'd like to read. Sylvia Plath comes to mind, as well as John Ciardi. Oh, and I'd love some e.e. cummings, particularly "Buffalo Bill." And there is a contemporary poet who has a collective book titled *Scrambled Eggs and Whiskey*, but for my life I can't recall his name.

I am including a poem I have been working on. I did a sort of Marcia trick. I found a short list of Latin phrase translations, went through and picked one for a title, then wrote a poem to suit it. More to follow. For now, I will close, always eager to return to your company.

Justin

September 10, 2010

Dear Marcia,

Just got a "two-fer" of letters from you loaded with goodies as usual. First of all, you brightened J.R.'s life a little with your poem. It is so wonderfully written, I cannot understand your own criticism of it. I have no trouble at all differentiating between the girl the hatted man loves, and the other one who loves him. Classic triangle, beautifully written. When I discussed it with him (simple fellow, remember?), he said, "Just like *Urban Cowboy*."

I don't recall that movie all that well, but I am guessing there was a similar dynamic in its plot. I love it when people who aren't supposed to "get it" go right for the important stuff of poetry; it proves it's universal. Of course, those movie guys have millions of dollars and two hours to make the same point.

Also, thanks for sending the West Memphis Three stuff. Sparked wonderful conversations here. Did I tell you at one time Echols was in Craighead County Jail while I was in there? Also, I talked with guys here who had done time in prison with the others. Nobody who ever spoke with them (at least in person) believes those boys are guilty. Oddly, convicts tend to be the biggest doubters of other convicts, but not in this case.

So glad you enjoyed *The Road*, I was the same way. Truly a dismal plot, and canned ending but brilliant despite that for his use of language. One of those peculiar things happened, they made a movie based on his book (and I guess the success of *No Country For Old Men*) but I hadn't known it. They showed it last weekend—weird, huh? The problem was his beautifully descriptive language was gone, and the camera only captured the dismal gray.

I picked up *Sin Killer* by Larry McMurtry at the library (he also wrote *Lonesome Dove*). I haven't really gotten into it yet, but I have always enjoyed his stuff. I noticed they also have *Texasville* — I'll get that next time. I suppose the rain is over for awhile so it's back to the fields tomorrow. I really don't mind, it's actually kind of nice.

Justin

(A letter from one of Justin's fellow inmates, J.R.)
September 12, 2010

Miss Marcia,

I hope this letter finds you doing well and in great spirits. Stick *[Justin's street name]* has let me to read some of your writings, and to be frank, I couldn't put them down!! You have such an uncanny ability to bring a story to life. Truly, you are a literary giant.

I also want to thank you for the poem you sent me. It means so much. Stick told me that you hardly ever write anymore, with a pen, I mean, so to have your signature is so awesome. I consider it as your autograph.

Since being here, I found that I enjoy poetry, I'm just a simple person raised up in the foothills of the Ozarks, but to me, poetry is a universal language. It is such a beautiful form of expressing one's self and telling a story. I've written one while being here, though not as good as either you or Stick's, but it served its purpose. I hope that in the next correspondence with you, you will allow me to send it to you for you to give me some pointers and criticism if need be.

Well, in closing, I once again thank you for your poem and the pleasure I've had from reading them and your stories. I hope to hear from you again. Take care and God bless.

Your friend,
J.R.

[I chose to include this letter in part to show the influence on and caring for other prisoners Justin had during his jail and prison years. I also wanted to point out the command of language this man has. I spent several years in the mountains of Arkansas, and I know that this man's school bus was probably an old pickup truck with a homemade camper shell. This would have been required for the sometimes one-lane dirt roads it would have to travel and the low-water bridges it would have to cross (small streams that could only be forded during low-water periods). Still, under all conditions, the love of language remained constant in all classes of Arkansans.]

September 20, 2010

Dear Marcia,

So good to hear that things went swimmingly well at the Starving Artist Café.

Okay, about the parole thing, my "jacket" (a folder filled any/all relevant information) goes before the Parole Board on Oct. 13. This is already good news because they do not want me to go before them personally.

At that time, they will approve my parole pending a parole plan, i.e., a suitable place to live. I do not have to already have a job, but just be able to vocalize how I'll go about finding one and becoming a productive member of society.

If I can get into Hidden Creek Project (from the article you sent) that would be my first choice. I also still have the address of Maple Street House in North Little Rock, the place where _____ has a small house and works doing remodel work. That would be my second choice.

Finally, I would settle for the Lighthouse of FIRMfoundation or any one of a half a dozen seamy places that make a living taking advantage of recent parolees and the homeless, but chances are I won't stay long at all.

I'm sorry that J.R. has been moved. I fear he may lose his leg, they have taken him to the hospital, but I will hang on to your poem ("Miss Marcia") for him. By the way, I cheated and read and I was warmed once again by your writing. I will go for now, so I can get this in the mail before they pick it up.

I will see you in days that down to double digits — thanks for staying in touch.

     Love,
     Justin

On Becoming Miss Marcia

When did I become Miss Marcia
a preordained title dreaded by many?
My carpenter calls me that,
as does the young man at the hardware store.
The sound of it rings across generations,
a hymn (that will not be silenced)
to old-fashioned propriety.

When youth wishes to approach age
with gentle familiarity,
wanting to draw closer but with respect,
I do not rail against my newfound name.
It warms me like a mantle passed from
courageous yet tender shoulders.

To be dubbed Miss Marcia
does not put me on the shelf,
it lifts me to a pedestal.

September 20, 2010

Dear Marcia,

I was gifted a letter from you today, along with some of Sylvia Plath's words. It won't be much longer until Poetry Day — when exactly is that? I am so very eager to see how my poems did — I am as a child at Christmas time driven to search tops of closets in my parents' absence. Curiouser and curiouser like *Alice in Wonderland*.

I am glad you sent the bio along with the poetry. I admit ignorance concerning her life — thought always her poetry has been dark to me. It means so much to me to learn about the greatest poets and see how it affects their work.

Oh, have you heard of the "Poets' Loft" in Hot Springs? I've met a guy who goes on Wednesday nights for readings, etc. I guess they have a sort of "open mic" policy about who reads and I may go check it out sometime.

[The Poet's Loft is the longest-running consecutive Wednesday night poetry meeting of its kind in the United States.]

_____ is certainly welcome to use any/all of my poetry she would like. Also, it would not bother/offend me if she said anything about my life/experiences. I am neither shy nor sensitive about those things. I would rather she read "Where we all sleep," but if she prefers "We Talked of Coleridge," it doesn't matter to me. I am pleased that she even thought to include anything that I have written.

Justin

September 24, 2010

Dear Marcia,

Did I ever mention that I have often eaten at Quapaw *[Quapaw Quarter Methodist Church at 17th and Louisiana in Little Rock, Arkansas]* and that is by far the finest hour of the week on the tramp trail? Each Sunday morning, from all over downtown, street people begin moving toward Quapaw. It is a sort of amazing time, at least in my mind. Most everyone knows each other, but the difference of a "flop," "shimmy," or "camp" of just a few blocks might keep them from seeing each other for several days.

Sundays most everyone is sober, and the atmosphere is close to a family reunion. They open the doors early, prepare two huge urns of coffee, warm leftover pastries from Starbucks, and have Sunday newspapers set about on tables.

The homeless come early and visit, read the paper and make plans. Sometimes, the church will have clean socks, some used clothes, or in the winter, warm gloves. Finally, a wonderful meal of scrambled eggs, biscuits and sausage gravy, fresh fruit and juice or milk is served. Most people go through the line at least twice though once is a big meal (if you've eaten lately).

Lots of times the serving is done by cherubic children who make me feel a little weepy with their eagerness to assist the dirty-faced crowd. One of the house guys at Serenity Park told me his mother "worked" Sundays at Quapaw. It is the kind of place that knows, for sure, how to give humanity back to the homeless — by far, more important than pastries.

It might interest you to know that there are at least two others from the downtown homeless scene here at Grimes. _____, a black man who pushes a shopping cart about, and _____, whom I mentioned in "Second and Cross." I let him read it when I got here, and he beamed, you wouldn't have thought I'd eulogized him in biography, instead I only said he was peeing behind a dumpster. I think just because it was so personal, and he knew everyone else, that made him happy.

I guess I'll close — oh, I saw an article in the paper about an 'over-the-jumps carousel' — it made me think of the unique merry-go-round in Little Rock's Fair Park, which is one of only two in existence on which horses go up and down and also feel like they are going "over the jumps."

Justin

October 6, 2010

Dear Marcia,

As I write, I am enjoying a cup of coffee, National Public Radio, and an evasive stillness not often found in this place. The weather has cooled, and lately we have been shelling peas, of course a much easier duty. It seems that for the moment all is well with the universe.

I was able to lay my hands on a book of interviews done with author John Cheever, who wrote *The Falconer* and dozens of short stories for *The New Yorker*. I really had never heard of him, but it was still great to hear what he had to say about writing and the process. Coincidentally, he had been an alcoholic for much of his life. The early conversations were colored by his drunkenness. Nearly every one of the interviews mentioned the bottle of Scotch that was always present. At a point in the late '70s, he quit drinking, and that is when he wrote *The Falconer*, it seems his best. I glean from the book that it is about a prison *[Cheever taught creative writing in Sing Sing Correctional Facility for a period]*, but only as a metaphor for addiction. I will see if I can find a copy come December.

At the same time, I found that one (the Cheever book), I picked up a text book that looks as though it is from an Intro to Journalism course, titled simply *Reporting*. I have been reading it as a sort of preparation for future writing. It had an interesting chapter on alternative/underground press that first drew my attention, but now I am reading it straight through.

Can hardly wait to read *The Choiring of The Trees* by Donald Harington, he was writing popularly at the time when the "nice" writers began to have more obvious (clumsy) sexual scenes and was emphatic that "one could not sell pornography," but I'd say that he probably missed the mark with that comment. As you know, I am far from prudish, but I think the physical act itself is handled with a heavy hand in pop fiction sometimes.

You may have noticed that I have not written much since I've been here, at least in this barracks, it is hardly conducive to writing to live in the throng of people that are present in an open barracks. I managed to write one though and will send it along before it is lost. Not quite satisfied somehow, but too loud to tweak out details — will tend to those later.

Justin

October 21, 2010

Marcia!

I have been informed of my forthcoming release! I have been approved for parole and with no stipulations!

I am so very happy, it looks as if by Christmas I will be home (to Little Rock). I am pleased you sent the copy of certificates and checks, my first "earnings" as a poet. I was pleased to see that the winner of the big prize was a really good poem and I'm sure that those others who placed were great, too. I hope everyone from the River Market group had a great time. I hope I never miss another as long as I live!

My mind races with all that I would like to do — sometimes waking me up in the middle of the night.

I have waited too late to write more, but I wanted to share my joyful news with you.

                                        Justin

Haunted (by Justin Booth)

His Pa long gone, mama frazzled and
busy pulling cockleburs
that refused to make way for
white tufted King Cotton, her nights
keeping shotgun shack spotless, and smelling
of neck bones and soup beans, finally
Top Jimmy scripture lit by coal oil lamp.

Nobody cared that the bastard
son of a suitcase sundry salesman
wandered, shiftless, down back roads
hot, sunbaked sand squishing between his toes,
dressed in worn overalls, shiny at the knees,
listening to mid-row field hand voices
rising even as backs bent. Old slave songs
so sad that he felt unalone.

When he was almost a man, angst
gave way to anger fueled by clear homemade
liquor, the cotton patches of Black Oak
could no longer contain him.
In Memphis, he held a mulatto girl dear,
but she laughed and called him boy.
He hit her and she fell shimmy limp.

So he fled back across the river,
stealing chickens all the way to Little Rock
and started capitol life as a stick-up kid.
After a pinch and a nickel at the Walls,
he went right back to the life and shot a
man while robbing an Esso station.
When he pulled the pistol, the fellow
with the bow tie and greasy finger nails had smirked.

By the time he left the general population
of Tucker State Pen, moving into Two Barracks
with seven other men who shared
Death Row — two rows of four cells
and of course Old Sparky.,
he had hand picked an ugly green tattoo
that read Ma into his forearm
with a safety pin wrapped in thread.

He had also suffered whippings at the
hands of redneck guards with wide leather belts
and been sodomized by a sneering
man named Chick and two
flunkies who laughed every time
he cried out in pain and humiliation.
The nightmares of his life haunted him
each night like shadows, unrelenting.

His neighbor, Pop, whose disembodied voice
thick as sorghum molasses, helpful and kind,
told stories of the ghosts that Old Sparky
had let loose to wander in eternal unrest.
The raspy shackles dragging or soul-piercing screams.
Everyone on the row heard and knew
they were real.

Pop was set next to fry. Sleep was not easy,
Spectral tales told through low vents on graffito walls
next to toilet bowls, filled the time.
Black Oak's own son sat Indian style on cold concrete
floor and shuddered —
no relief in sight, no rest for the wicked.

The unit, secured twenty-three hours a day,
echoed with successive slamming steel door sounds.

Sometimes the bare lights dimmed as if
the sizzle chair had just made love to another.
The bulls came and shaved Pops cotton-top locks.
The oily voice in the vent was quiet that night.

Whether the glitch was an act of sadism
by guards or poltergeist, Pop was being tortured.
His normal pitch thick voice rising,
"Mo' juice, God Almighty, mo' juice,"
writhing in restraints like a spring slug
on salted sidewalk,
"Sweet Baby Jesus, mo' juice,"
finally giving up the ghost.

Alone again with the ghosts of his past

>   with the smirking, bow-tied Esso man,

>   with the high-yellow girl he would have loved,

>   with the absent father who'd sinned with his
>   mother

>   with the sounds of clanging steel and the ghastly
>   smell that reminded him of his schoolmate
>   falling,
> hands out, into the Franklin stove years ago.

The gust of breeze that accompanied the opening of his
    tumble-locked steel door, cool
on the freshly shorn scalp, he rose and became
the dead man walking, shuffling between the uniformed
    Angels of Death and strapping in,
alone again for the last switch thrown moment.

Alone.

ABOUT MARCIA CAMP

Photo by Angela Camp Dyke

Marcia Camp turned down two journalism scholarships because, she says, "Formal education would have robbed me of my ability to think outside the box. It was the best decision I ever made."

Her essays, profiles, short stories and poetry have appeared in journals, books and periodicals across the country. "The subject matter that interests me sometimes calls for the breadth of prose, other times the penetrating depth of poetry. For me, subject determines form."

The self-help book, *You Can't Leave Till You Do the Paperwork*, appeared in 1999. *The Charity Letters of JoAnn Cayce*, an in-depth look at the unbelievable poverty in the rural Delta, was published in 2008. *Still Driving on the Sidewalk*, a collection of published essays, will be available later this year.

Visit us at
cowbudpub.com

This title is also available as an e-book.

www.ingramcontent.com/pod-product-compliance
Lightning Source LLC
Chambersburg PA
CBHW051701040426
42446CB00009B/1242